WILLIAM

A Royal Love Story

& KATE

HarperCollins*Publishers*
77–85 Fulham Palace Road,
Hammersmith, London W6 8JB

www.harpercollins.co.uk

First published by HarperCollins*Publishers* in 2010 in association with News Group Newspapers, a subsidiary of News International Limited

The Sun and *The Sun* Logo are registered trademarks of News Group Newspapers Limited

Visit *The Sun* website at www.thesun.co.uk

10 9 8 7 6 5 4 3 2 1

All images are courtesy of *The Sun*, with the following exceptions:

p34, 78, 91 AFP; p4, 141, 178 AFP/Getty; p68, 189 Alamy; p82 All Action Digital; p51 Alpha; p28, 36 AP; p193, 201, 208 Arthur Edwards/*The Sun*; p94 Barcroft Media; p98 Big Pictures; p20, 29 Corbis; p114 Desmond O'Neill; p135 Enigma; p146, 150 EPA; p200 Eyevine; p158, 167 Getty; p154 Goff Photos; p148 Jim Bennett; p117, 122, 123 Matrix; p71, 99, 101, 110, 133, 151, 153, 170, 175, 196 News Group Newspapers; p142 Newspix; p7, 10, 39, 40, 55, 83, 90, 92, 102, 105, 128, 161, 166 PA; p41, 42 Peter Kelly; p136 Peter Nicholls; p25, 48, 62, 76, 113, 119, 153, 159, 162, 172 Reuters; p23, 44, 74, 109, 125, 141, 144, 145, 164, 166, 168, 169 Rex Features; p120, 154 Solarpix; p54 Splash; p61 *Daily Mail*; p14, 85, 87, 88, 126, 129, 130, 132, 185 Times Newspapers Limited; p126 Woolworths; p18 WPA Solo Rota; p30 Xposure

A catalogue record of this book is available from the British Library

ISBN 978-0-00-739380-0

Printed and bound in Great Britain by
Butler, Tanner and Dennis Ltd, Frome, Somerset

Mixed Sources
Product group from well-managed forests and other controlled sources
www.fsc.org Cert no. SW-COC-001806
© 1996 Forest Stewardship Council

FSC

FSC is a non-profit international organisation established to promote the responsible management of the world's forests. Products carrying the FSC label are independently certified to assure consumers that they come from forests that are managed to meet the social, economic and ecological needs of present and future generations.

Find out more about HarperCollins and the environment at
www.harpercollins.co.uk/green

Contents

Introduction

The outpouring of joy at the news of Prince William's long-awaited engagement to the beautiful Kate Middleton should come as no surprise to anyone. William has always held a special place in the hearts of the British people, who have recognised qualities in Kate that make her a perfect future Queen.

Patriotic supporters of the Royal Family have closely followed every twist and turn of William's life as though he were a favourite nephew or the son of a best friend. During his teenage years, there was an enduring fascination over who he would choose to become his wife. *The Sun* was the first newspaper to tell the world that William had fallen in love with Kate. From that day on, the public paid close attention to the shapely brunette and were charmed by everything they saw. The national obsession over William's love life subtly shifted from 'Who?' to the pressing question of 'When?'

In finally asking Kate to marry him, William is set to wed a young woman who boasts a winning combination of glamour, grace, poise

and intelligence. Many believe that she will now enchant us in the same way as her future husband's late mother, the immensely popular and beguiling Princess Diana. Those who have closely monitored the couple's relationship are convinced that they make a better match than Diana and Prince Charles, William's father. A mere six months separates them in age rather than the 12-year gulf that divided Charles and Diana. They share similar interests, character traits and a healthy desire for normality in spite of their unique circumstances.

Yet in almost every way, their backgrounds could not be more different—as you would expect from a union between a young man born to be King and a girl from the Home Counties.

'William is set to wed a young woman who boasts a winning combination of glamour, grace, poise and intelligence.'

1

Worlds Apart

With every imaginable privilege available to him and flunkies on hand to attend to his every whim, William should have enjoyed a dream upbringing. But ironically it was Kate who had the more enviable start in life, basking in the warmth of her family's stability, security and love.

Catherine Elizabeth Middleton was born on 9 January 1982, to mum Carole and dad Michael in Reading's Royal Berkshire Hospital. Just over eighteen months later she was joined by a sister, Pippa, and, three and a half years after that, a brother James arrived. Carole Goldsmith was working as an air hostess in the 1970s when she met her man. Michael Middleton was a pilot whose powerful masculine looks made him very popular amongst female flight attendants. After a brief time dating, Michael and Carole married in Chiltern, Buckinghamshire, in 1980.

Kate was born two years later and spent the first 13 years of her life growing up in the village of West View, near Bradfield Southend, Berkshire. Her parents had bought the four-bed semi-detached Victorian villa for £35,000 in 1979 – and it was from here that they made a very important life decision. It is one that has almost certainly contributed to Kate's position today. They were determined to give everything to their children and agreed that international jet-setting was not compatible with family life. They left the airline industry to set up Party Pieces, a mail-order company supplying packs of goodies to guarantee the perfect kids' bash. Appropriately, wedding kits and princess costumes are amongst the items now shipped by the family firm's successful online operation.

In 1987, Carole launched the business from a back-garden shed, later expanding into a small industrial unit in nearby Yattendon. Eight years on, the growing firm moved base again into converted farm buildings a mile down the road. In the same year, the family paid £250,000 for a home in the village of Bucklebury. The five-bedroom detached property set within woodland is now worth more than £1 million.

Kate experienced an idyllic childhood, growing up in picture-postcard English villages with parents who packaged and sold fun for a living. A blog she wrote on the Party Pieces website years later provides a telling insight into her carefree youth. She portrayed herself as a happy and outgoing child who loved to dress up as a clown in giant dungarees at fancy dress parties. She described her best party memory as 'an amazing white rabbit marshmallow cake that Mummy made when I was seven'. Musical statues, she revealed, was a favourite game because she had 'always been a keen dancer'. Party bags were best, she said, when they contained 'anything that Mummy would normally never allow me to have. They were always such a treat.' She recommended cooking parties for girls and camping parties for boys because they were 'a great way to get Daddies involved'. And she admitted she

had suffered a 'cake disaster' during James's birthday when she forgot to add self-raising flour and turned a flat sponge into a trifle cake.

When William and Kate speak about their respective childhoods, her innocent memories must seem a million miles from some of his painful recollections. His youth was blighted by the trauma of his parents' marriage breakdown and the tragically premature death of his mother — all played out in the media spotlight.

Life began promisingly enough for Prince William Arthur Philip Louis Wales, the boy destined one day to become the 42nd monarch since William the Conqueror took the English throne in 1066. His birth at St Mary's Hospital in London on 21 June 1982 was met with a 41-gun salute, the sounding of bells and rejoicing that reverberated around Britain and beyond. It came 11 months after Prince Charles, the Queen's eldest son, had tied the knot with the then Lady Diana Spencer.

Their fairy-tale ceremony at St Paul's Cathedral was watched by a worldwide audience of 750 million people who were transfixed by the pomp and pageantry.

'Diana made it her mission to give them a sense of fun, freedom and – most importantly – normality.'

William inherited his mother's good looks, his father's inquiring nature and — as the passing years would reveal — the House of Windsor hairline. Prince Harry was born just over two years after William, and the two were to become close friends and allies.

They were brought up in palatial surroundings, with nanny Barbara Barnes keeping a watchful eye over them in their early years.

Being a Prince certainly had many advantages over being a commoner. William once received a £60,000 scaled-down Jaguar car for his birthday, making Kate's clown dungarees look rather small beer in comparison. On another occasion, he jokingly threatened a school rival with his grandmother's soldiers during a row.

But as he got older, there was no hiding from the fact that his parents' marriage was collapsing in front of his — and the nation's — eyes. Whoever was to blame for the relationship's failure — and everyone had an opinion — there was universal sympathy for William and Harry when Charles and Diana split in 1992. At an age when Kate was playing musical statues, William was caught in the middle of a brutal separation that infamously contributed to the Queen's 'annus horribilis'.

In spite of this, even Charles and Diana's worst critics would concede that individually they had done their very best for their sons. Diana made it her mission to give them a sense of fun, freedom and — most importantly — normality. Charles was determined that they

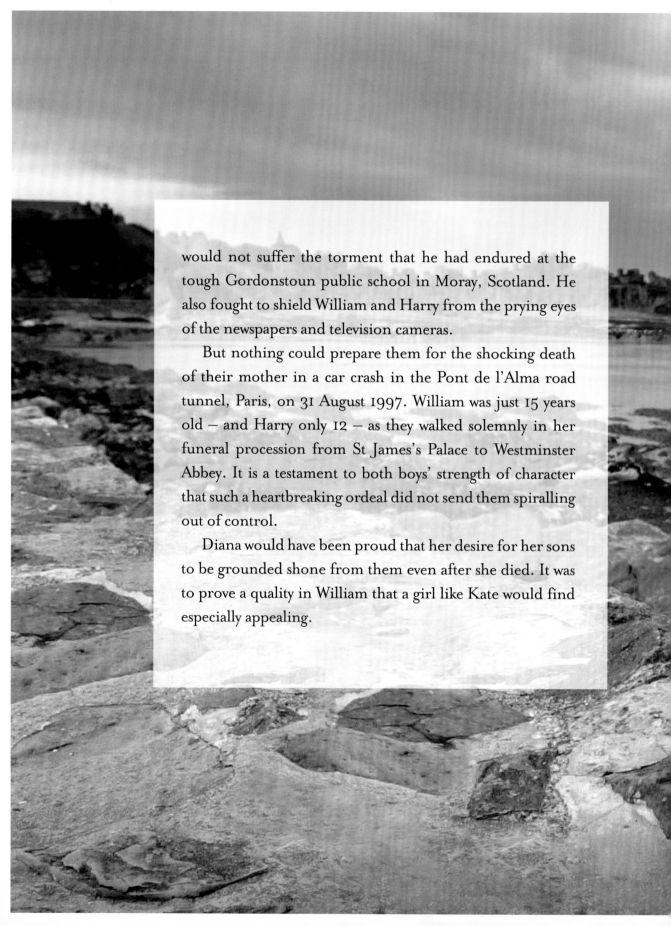

would not suffer the torment that he had endured at the tough Gordonstoun public school in Moray, Scotland. He also fought to shield William and Harry from the prying eyes of the newspapers and television cameras.

But nothing could prepare them for the shocking death of their mother in a car crash in the Pont de l'Alma road tunnel, Paris, on 31 August 1997. William was just 15 years old — and Harry only 12 — as they walked solemnly in her funeral procession from St James's Palace to Westminster Abbey. It is a testament to both boys' strength of character that such a heartbreaking ordeal did not send them spiralling out of control.

Diana would have been proud that her desire for her sons to be grounded shone from them even after she died. It was to prove a quality in William that a girl like Kate would find especially appealing.

2

A Schoolgirl Crush

Carole and Michael Middleton were utterly determined to give Kate, Pippa and James the best possible start in life. The burgeoning success of Party Pieces provided them with the necessary funds to invest in a private education for their children. From the age of 4 to 12, Kate was sent to St Andrew's prep school in Pangbourne, Berkshire. This £10,000-a-year institution was just a few miles from the family home in Bucklebury, and, as far as her development was concerned, it wasn't long before the hefty fees seemed to pay off.

She immersed herself in school life. Kate was one of the most popular and successful pupils at St Andrew's. In the school magazine, *The Chronicle*, her achievements were splashed across most pages. She was a tennis champion and the captain of the rounders, netball, cross-country and swimming teams. The sports master showered her with praise when he wrote of her hockey skills:

She is a quick and talented player, although at times she can be erratic...

And in athletics, she held both the long and high jump school records. A former St Andrew's pupil recalls: 'Kate was so sporty. In many ways she was a real tomboy and the teachers loved her.'

Her talents stretched beyond the sports field and into amateur dramatics. In 1993, *The Chronicle* records her appearance as a Junior Rat in a school production of *Ratz*. Later that year, she took the lead part of Eliza Doolittle in the classic *My Fair Lady*. According to *The Chronicle* of June 1994, Kate 'glided about the stage looking stylish and serene'. It was not surprising that she was rewarded for all her work, winning that year's prize for 'all-round effort and pleasantness'. Her friend added: 'She was a model pupil. In fact she was from a model family. Her parents were really supportive of all three children. They regularly got involved with the school and a lot of the girls even had a bit of a crush on Kate's dad Michael. They were really down to earth, a normal happy family, and the stability undoubtedly rubbed off on Kate. She was very mature for her age and things just didn't seem to bother her in the way that they did everyone else.'

Kate left St Andrew's at 11 to attend Downe House in Newbury, where she spent two apparently unhappy years. She then transferred to the exclusive £26,000-a-year Marlborough College in Wiltshire, where she boarded in Elmhurst House.

In February 1998, a rumour bounced off the mixed public school's corridors the day before a hockey match. The excited chattering was loudest amongst the female students. 'He's coming here – he's actually coming here,' they shrieked. 'And better still, he'll be wearing shorts!' By the time 'he' finally arrived, the banks around Marlborough's hockey pitches were packed with pupils determined to catch their first glimpse of Prince William.

The young Prince had attended the pre-prep Wetherby School in Notting Hill, West London, followed by Ludgrove School in Wokingham, Berkshire. From there, he passed the entrance exams for the world-renowned Eton College - an achievement that delighted his father, who saw it as infinitely preferable to his old school, Gordonstoun. And it was the hockey team from Eton that was due to take on Marlborough for the annual inter-school fixture.

Former pupils at Marlborough are unlikely to remember the final score. But few of those who watched the game will ever forget the day they saw William up close. Yet not a single person crammed onto the rain-sodden sidelines realised what they were actually witnessing. That muddy match produced one of the most important moments in modern Royal history. Hidden amongst the hordes of admiring young girls was, of course, the 16-year-old Kate Middleton.

It was the first time William's bride-to-be had clapped eyes on the man she would one day marry.

A fellow schoolmate recalled the air of anticipation surrounding the game. She said: 'Like all of us Kate was excited. She wasn't a shy girl at school but at the same time she was far more level-headed than most of her classmates. Several of them were almost hysterical about seeing Prince William in the flesh. Everyone wanted to catch his eye or, better still, get to talk to him. A few of the girls even put on make-up and made a special effort with their hair in the hope of making an impression. But Kate was above all that. As ever, she just played it cool and came with us to watch.'

'She was a model pupil... Her parents were really supportive of all three children.'

Sadly, the heavens opened and the day didn't quite play out as many of the Marlborough girls had hoped. The school chum remembered: 'In the end, we all got soaked and none of us got to speak to William. Looking back, it seems amazing that William and Kate would eventually end up together.'

Seeing the second-in-line to the throne in the flesh apparently confirmed the schoolgirl crush Kate had harboured for some time.

Another former school friend, Jessica Hay, who knew Kate as Catherine, said: 'Another girl predicted Catherine would fall in love with a prince. She would tell Catherine that one day she would be the Queen of England - and she would shriek in disbelief.'

Jessica said that Kate was jokingly known to pals as 'princess-in-waiting' and insisted that William would be her first serious boyfriend. Racy Kate also occasionally joined in with wilder spirits by mooning out of the window as goggle-eyed lads strolled past. Jessica said: 'One night I told her to just do it and she did. She would have been 14 at the time.'

Kate is now known to the public by her trademark glossy chestnut hair, stylish dress sense and confident manner. But this was not always the case. In fact Kate - known to some at school as 'Middi' - was the most unlikely of girls to catch a prince's eye. Plain but popular, she continued to excel at sport and was 'solid' academically but did not tick the boxes of a potential princess-in-waiting.

Other more suitable candidates were growing up in stately homes, polishing their nails along with their manners. But while they were learning how to behave within the upper classes, Kate was different.

It was only in her last year at Marlborough that Kate finally began blossoming into a confident young woman. She also hit her academic stride, following her high-grade passes in 11 GCSEs with three good A-levels. The friend said: 'She went to a party just a few weeks before her A-levels and she was the one girl all the guys wanted to chat up. She was tanned, had an athletic body and lovely legs - basically they all lusted after her. Even the way she talked had changed. Her accent

had become more posh and it was as though she was trying to shake off those middle-class roots.'

William, meanwhile, gained A-levels in geography, history of art and biology, respectively scoring A, B and C grades. Then - just like Kate and thousands of other well-heeled students - he embarked on a gap year. He would enjoy many memorable experiences, including a safari in Africa, volunteer work in Chile and grafting as a farm labourer in England.

He had no doubt long since forgotten about the hockey match against Marlborough. But while he may not have spotted Kate that day, he would get to see a whole lot more of her at his next educational waypoint.

'Her accent had become more posh and it was as though she was trying to shake off those middle-class roots.'

Girl on the Bus

Kate endeared herself to the public after she was spotted travelling on a bus. She took the number 19 from Chelsea into the West End on a shopping trip in October 2005. Six months later she was snapped waiting for the number 137 in Sloane Square after enjoying a lunch with her mum.

One onlooker said: 'At the bus stop she completely blended in and certainly did not stand out from the crowd.' She wore sunglasses for the second outing and wasn't disturbed by other passengers.

Her lawyers Harbottle & Lewis were unhappy about the pictures and complained that her privacy was being invaded. But the British people were charmed — a possible future Queen free from airs and graces, and using public transport.

Maybe she should have stuck to buses for a little while longer. In October 2008, she was snapped talking on her mobile phone while driving — but wasn't prosecuted.

3

Catwalk Queen

The air of excitement around the University of St Andrews was palpable as the new intake of first years arrived in autumn 2001. For the young men already attending the esteemed establishment in Fife on the east coast of Scotland, it meant plentiful supplies of pretty fresher girls ripe for chatting up. But for the female students it signified something else altogether: Prince William, the world's most eligible bachelor, was about to hit town.

It was a matter of weeks since New York's Twin Towers had collapsed in a shocking terrorist attack, but William's imminent appearance still dominated many conversations. His decision to enrol on a history of art degree had sparked unprecedented interest in Scotland's oldest uni. An incredible surge in applications – a 44 per cent increase on the usual number – thunked with deafening inevitability onto the admissions office mat. Many were from husband-hunting US society girls, each of them dreaming of landing a British Royal. All 130 places on the four-year course were snapped up within hours of the news that the young Prince had, somewhat unsurprisingly, been granted his place.

Kate Middleton – fit, fresh and ready to study after her gap year in Italy and South America – was amongst their number.

William skipped Freshers' Week, the traditionally boozy opening days of university life, in a bid to avoid handing the press a field day. 'It would have been a media frenzy and that's not fair on the other new students,' he said. 'Plus I thought I would probably end up in a gutter, completely wrecked, and the people I had met that week wouldn't end up being my friends anyway.' He added with some candour: 'It also meant I could have another week's holiday.'

The casually dressed Prince was finally dropped off at St Andrews after being driven there by Prince Charles in a green Vauxhall Omega estate. He was greeted by the principal Dr Brian Lang, 4,000 well-wishers and a group of protesters venting their feelings over the looming war in Afghanistan. William shook the hands of those there to welcome him and seemed refreshingly convinced that the level of interest in him would rapidly subside. 'It will be easier as time goes on,' he said. 'Everyone will get bored of me, which they do.'

Home for the next academic year would be a £2,273-a-year en-suite room in St Salvator's hall of residence - affectionately known as St Sally's - with protection officers in rooms on either side of him. As fate would have it, Kate had only just finished unpacking her bags inside her new digs on a different floor of the same mixed college.

As earnestly as William hoped that his peers would 'get bored' of him, it was a mere matter of days before controversy erupted.

Students complained of an uninvited and unwanted film crew lurking in the shadows of the old town's streets. Palace aides had brokered a deal with the media that they believed would guarantee

William privacy while he was in higher education. To hear that it was being flouted so flagrantly and so early in his studies enraged them.

Then, to the complete disbelief of all concerned – but especially to William and his dad – it emerged that the camera team had a Royal link. They had been sent by Ardent Productions, the TV company run by Prince Edward, Charles's youngest brother and William's uncle. Understandably, the young Prince was livid at the betrayal and rang his dad to complain. Charles made his feelings known to Edward in no uncertain terms.

The episode made for an uncomfortable start to William's new life and set an unhappy tone that would characterize his first year. While he was ultimately allowed freedom to breathe by the rest of the world's media, he found St Andrews claustrophobic. He was also finding his history of art course a boring grind and, in common with many homesick first-year undergraduates, missed his school friends and family.

'Palace aides had brokered a deal with the media that they believed would guarantee William privacy while he was in higher education.'

THE PRIVACY DEAL

William and Kate's love affair was able to thrive at St Andrews because of a deal between Clarence House, Lord Wakeham of the Press Complaints Commission, and the media.

The young Prince had completed his school days at Eton and his gap year abroad free from photographers' lenses. His first ever official engagement with his father was to attend the PCC's 10th anniversary party as a way of showing his appreciation to Fleet Street editors. But he feared that all bets were off at St Andrews and worried that his life could turn into a free-for-all.

The subject was a particularly sensitive one after the circumstances surrounding his mother's death. A drunken driver may have been to blame for the Paris crash, but William would under-standably never forget that she was being pursued by paparazzi.

In fact, another gentlemen's agreement was reached that seemed to keep both sides happy. William would give occasional carefully managed interviews at landmark moments in his life – such as his 21st birthday – in which limited photo opportunities were granted. In return, news teams would stay away from the halls of residence, the campus and the town. Two days before William arrived at the university, the PCC and Andrew Neil – former editor of *The Sunday Times* and now rector of St Andrews – held a meeting with 400 students. They were informed that they would also be protected from any prying eyes. Students were later warned that anyone found leaking information about William would be kicked out. Newspapers and broadcasters were told they could cover William's arrival at the university as long as they were out of town by nightfall.

The agreement got off to a shaky start – William was late after lunch with the Queen Mother at Birkhall on the Balmoral estate. Incredibly, Prince Edward's Ardent Productions team hung around, only to be humiliatingly booted off site days later.

But that was the sole – albeit extraordinary – blip in a media deal which William later hailed as a success. 'There's lots of people saying it's impossible to lead a normal life really,' he said. 'But actually up here, and with the media out of it, it's amazing how folk just get on with their lives and will not bother you.'

The one bright spot in an apparently downbeat existence was that he had made some new chums. And it was Kate, the pretty brunette he saw regularly on his course and in his halls, who was very much a key player in this developing set.

Overcoming their shared natural shyness, they gravitated towards each other through a number of other mutual interests.

Over a coffee in the halls of residence – or perhaps something stronger at local bars such as Ma Bells or The Gin House – they would excitedly recount their respective gap-year experiences of Chile. They both a shared love of sport – he played rugby, polo, water polo and enjoyed skiing – and their burgeoning friendship strengthened across the tennis net. But it was nothing more than that – a platonic relation-ship – in those early days at St Andrews.

Kate dated charming older law student Rupert Finch for some months, while William briefly stepped out with fellow fresher Carley Massy-Birch. William's views on potential university girlfriends became clear more than 18 months later, when he gave an interview to mark his 21st birthday at the end of his second year in June 2003.

He said that he didn't have a 'steady girlfriend' but insisted that it wasn't through a lack of confidence. 'If I fancy a girl and I really like her and she fancies me back, which is rare, I ask her out,' he said. 'But, at the same time, I don't want to put them in an awkward situa-tion because a lot of people don't quite understand what comes with knowing me, for one, and secondly, if they were my girlfriend, the excitement it would probably cause.'

He also expressed his frustration and bewilderment at the level of intense scrutiny that surrounded his love life. 'There's been a lot of speculation about every single girl I'm with and it actually does quite irritate me after a while, more so because it's a complete pain for the girls,' he admitted. 'These poor girls, you know, whom I've either just met and get photographed with, or they're friends of mine, suddenly get thrown into the limelight and their parents get rung up and so on. I think it's a little unfair on them really. I'm used to it because it happens quite a lot now. But it's very difficult for them and I don't like that at all.' And he joked:

'Only the mad girls chase me. No, I've never been aware of anyone chasing me but if there were, could they please leave their telephone number.'

Kate was neither mad nor chasing William, but she had his mobile number.

She was close enough to the future King by the end of the first term to act as a valued confidante when he hit his lowest ebb at St Andrews. He was unsettled and making regular 900-mile round trips to Prince Charles's Highgrove estate near Tetbury in Gloucestershire.

Over the Christmas holidays, he told his father that enough was enough and he wanted to quit the university.

This presented a potential PR disaster for the Royal Family and would draw unflattering comparisons with Prince Edward's failure to stick with the Royal Marines 15 years earlier. After consulting with aides, Prince Charles took a tough line with his elder son. He sat him down and told him quitting was not an option.

'He didn't think that watching his attractive new friend would prove to be much of a chore – and he was right.'

William returned in January, under no illusion that he must show his mettle. His spirits were given a massive boost in March of his second term when he heard that Kate was to model in a college fashion show. William bought a £200 VIP front-row seat to lend his support at the event, which was called 'Don't Walk' and sponsored by Yves St Laurent.

He didn't think that watching his attractive new friend would prove to be much of a chore - and he was right. Kate was the shining star of the show. She drew gasps of admiration as she sashayed along the catwalk wearing a sheer black lace dress over a strapless bra and black bikini bottoms. The daring outfit showed off Kate's toned frame to perfection and William watched agog as he saw her in a completely new light. Just four years on from the Eton vs Marlborough hockey match, a total role reversal had taken place. It was now William who couldn't take his eyes off Kate.

He respected her judgment, too. Following chats with Kate and his tutors, he decided to switch courses to geography after struggling to get to grips with history of art. With the academic cloud that had been hanging over his head lifting, a high-spirited William set about looking for a flat to rent for his second year. He would share with old Etonian pal Fergus Boyd and - of course - his very good friend Kate Middleton.

4

From Housemates to Dates

William and Kate returned to start their second year by moving into a £400-a-week luxury Edwardian townhouse with Fergus and another female friend. The £600,000 property was situated in one of St Andrews' most sought-after Georgian streets, where well-to-do students regularly held boisterous garden parties.

During the summer, Kate had found that media interest in her as William's easy-on-the-eye future housemate was cranking up. She took a job as a barmaid to clear some student debts, only to discover that her boss was babbling to the papers. Rory Laing ran the posh catering firm 'Snatch' and would later make a brief appearance in the popular BBC reality show *The Apprentice*. He had hired Kate to serve Pimm's at the Henley Royal Regatta and spoke highly of her. 'As we only employ former public school pupils, she fits our profile brilliantly,' he told a diary column. 'I pay Kate only £5.25 an hour but she's a pretty girl, so she takes home plenty in tips.'

Despite their privileged backgrounds, the close chums were happy to live like normal undergraduates in their new student home. William had enjoyed the option of three meals a day while in St Salvator's and now relied heavily on takeaway curries for sustenance. But he also joined Kate to stock up on food at supermarkets Safeway or Tesco, or to buy a bag of pick-and-mix sweets at Woolworths. 'I do all my own shopping,' he said in one interview about his student life. 'I go out to get takeaways, rent videos, go to the cinema, basically anything I want to, really. I've spent hours in the queues at Tesco. I haven't got to grips with the self-service.'

He sometimes cooked for Kate and his other housemates despite – by his own admission – not being the world's greatest chef. But life for William and Kate in the student house share wasn't all plain sailing. Dirty dishes became a bone of contention until the quartet pooled resources and shelled out for a dishwasher. William said later: 'Before, it was a complete disaster. There would be piles and piles left in the sink, and one of us would come back in and immediately walk out when they saw it. It would just get bigger and bigger. It would never get done. The amount of arguments about washing up and cleaning or whatever. It still goes on but it's better now. It's the dynamics of living with people. When you all live together you've got to muck in and help out.'

Although largely happy to roam free in St Andrews, William sometimes cycled to college with a cap pulled over his face to shield his identity. Kate's ever-growing confidence emerged as she became the founder member of an all-girl society called the Lumsden Club. Its purpose was to raise awareness of women's issues, as well as cash for their charities, and to rival a controversial all-male club that had existed at the university for years.

Towards the end of William and Kate's enjoyable second year, *The Sun* became the first newspaper to reveal just how close they had

'Kate took a job as a barmaid to clear some student debts, only to discover that her boss was babbling to the papers.'

become. In May 2003, we ran the headline 'William's Special K' on our front page. Our story told how the couple's body language had given away their feelings for each other during a university rugby sevens tournament. William played in the competition and was cheered on by an enthusiastic Kate, whose relationship with Rupert was by now uncertain. William and Kate spent most of their free time flirting as they lay side by side in deep conversation. And they were happy to coo over each other, apparently oblivious to the presence of scores of onlookers.

One said: 'Their body language was very revealing. They looked very close. They seemed very intimate and I have no doubt they were together.'

A friend of Kate described her as 'very bubbly', adding, 'but she's also very discreet about William.'

Kate's dad Michael Middleton laughed off the story, and insisted that his daughter and the future King were 'just good friends'. 'People do not seem to realise that there are two girls and two boys sharing the flat at the university,' he said. 'They are together all the time because they're the best of pals – and yes, cameramen are going to get photos of them together.' In words that tend to suggest Party Pieces won't be marketing a range of crystal balls, he added: 'But there is nothing more to it than that. We are very amused at the thought of being in-laws to Prince William, but I don't think it is going to happen.'

No one doubted his sincerity. But had Kate yet confided in her parents about the strength of her feelings for William? Their firm friendship at the very least was not in doubt.

William quietly paid a visit to the Middleton family home for a summer party to celebrate Kate's 21st birthday – which had actually fallen months previously. He slipped into a marquee for the 1920s-themed bash and left immediately after finishing his dinner. It wasn't reported at the time, but its significance would emerge as other events unfolded.

Naturally enough, Kate had made the guest list for William's 21st birthday in June, the end of their second academic year together. She attended the *Out of Africa*-themed fancy dress bash at Windsor Castle, alongside other stunning young women who were considered possible future Queens. The double-barrelled babes included his polo-playing pal Natalie Hicks-Lobbecke and party-girl Davina Duckworth-Chad, who had once joined the Prince for a summer cruise.

WILLIAM'S 21ST BIRTHDAY, 21 JUNE 2003

Kate would never forget the night she first rubbed shoulders with the Royal Family at William's 21st birthday party inside Windsor Castle.

The Out of Africa-themed do gave the wide-eyed student the chance to see the Queen and Prince Philip at first hand ... and in fancy dress. Her Majesty wore an understated Queen of Swaziland outfit, while Prince Charles looked resplendent in a striped kaftan.

Many of William's friends from St Andrews had enjoyed privileged backgrounds like Kate, but this really was another world. Exotically costumed Royals exchanged pleasantries with the upper classes, including William's aunts and uncles on his mum's side, as well as former nannies, and rooms were adorned with 12ft-high model elephants, tribal masks and animal skins.

But Kate could never have predicted that the party would be remembered for a crazy intruder who could have wiped out the Monarchy at a stroke.

Crackpot comedian Aaron Barschak somehow slipped through the ring of steel thrown around the castle by police officers. William, bare-chested in a Tarzan loincloth, was on a stage occupied by a DJ and an African band when his party was hijacked at 11.20 pm.

He had just started to thank Prince Charles – dressed as a West African King – and the Queen for organising the party when Barschak sprang forward. Sporting a false beard and dressed in a salmon-pink ballgown, white turban, red shoes and dark glasses, he grabbed the mic. In a thick Arabic accent he started shouting out that his name was 'Osama' and mumbled some other words.

William frantically signalled to guards to remove him and he was taken away in handcuffs. Keeping cool under pressure, William quickly recovered his composure to tell guests: 'I didn't know my brother could do an accent like that.' Prince Harry witnessed the astonishing breach alongside his uncle Prince Andrew and cousins Princesses Beatrice and Eugenie.

The Queen was said to be 'furious' over the fiasco and William himself was livid.

Kate kept her thoughts to herself. But she must have wondered what she might be letting herself in for.

Also highly tipped as a potential wife was Jessica 'Jecca' Craig, the daughter of a wealthy Kenyan wildlife sanctuary owner. William had got on with Jecca like a house on fire when he stayed on her family's Lewa Downs nature reserve during part of his gap year.

She was guest of honour at the party but, despite talk of a pretend teen 'engagement' between them, he denied a romance. Unusually, Clarence House even went to the extent of issuing a statement denying a romance between William and Jecca. But the declaration served only to stir up more interest and she was still seen as a serious love rival to Kate. William shone in front of both girls when he handled a potentially explosive situation.

So-called 'comedy terrorist' Aaron Barschak had sneaked past security and grabbed the mic from William to make a speech. The young Prince simply gave his personal protection officer a nod, and weirdo Barschak was swiftly seized and ejected—although never charged with any offence.

At the start of their third year at St Andrews, William, Kate and Fergus moved from their townhouse into a country cottage. Only the two main players — and perhaps Fergus — know for definite the precise moment when friendship turned to love. But it seems certain that the 'Romance of the Millennium' had ignited by Christmas 2003.

The following March, William and Kate travelled from Scotland to North Yorkshire for the coincidentally named Middleton Hunt. William, it was said, had introduced Kate to some of his old crowd as 'my girlfriend'.

A month later, it was once again *The Sun* that stuck its neck on the line to keep the public up to speed with the fast-moving relationship. William and Kate WERE together, we announced, and it was serious.

Most tellingly, Kate had joined William at Highgrove at least three times and they had enjoyed weekend trysts at a remote cottage on the Queen's Balmoral estate. The bolthole had provided some much-needed space for them away from the St Andrews goldfish bowl. Fergus, we revealed, had been sworn to secrecy back at university and would discreetly make himself scarce to leave the couple alone in the cottage.

Or they would dine at The Doll's House restaurant, which was owned by the husband of TV's Carol Smillie.

A source said: 'It is true they are dating and try to spend as much time with each other as possible, but never in public.'

Prince Charles had also now been introduced to his son's girlfriend and was said to have signalled his approval.

The story broke as William and Kate skied with Prince Charles and other close friends in the favoured Royal resort of Klosters, Switzerland. These included Harry Legge-Bourke, the younger brother of William's former unofficial nanny Tiggy, as well as Guy Pelly, infamously – but wrongly – blamed for Prince Harry's drug taking. William van Cutsem, son of Prince Charles's friend Hugh, and van Cutsem's girlfriend Katie James made up the group.

William's press minders refused to confirm that the couple were dating, and other less well-informed newspapers rubbished our exclusive. Clarence House did not, however, pour cold water on the story, as they had done over the Jecca Craig rumours a year earlier. But they reacted heavy-handedly over the pictures of William and Kate that we printed. They banned legendary *The Sun* snapper Arthur Edwards from future official engagements – even though he hadn't taken the shots in question.

We responded by saying that the story was completely true and pointing out that there was a tremendous public interest in the pictures. Arthur himself insisted: 'I am disappointed, as I will be prevented from doing the job I love. Banning *The Sun* from any event involving

William and Harry is a silly, childish thing to do.'

The squabble was Kate's first real taste of how her life would be changing as William's girlfriend. But far from being overwhelmed by the social circles in which she was now moving, she displayed her growing feisty streak. When a friend told her that she was 'so lucky' to be dating William, she laughed: 'He's so lucky to be going out with me!'

Although they had made a pact to keep the affair secret, they struggled to hide their obvious affection on the slopes. And other connections were made by Royal watchers. William had been spotted kissing a girl with long dark hair at the water polo Christmas Ball the previous year. Had it been Kate? It seemed more than likely now.

They Are an Item:
How The Sun Broke the Story

In April 2004, *The Sun* scooped the world when we revealed that William and Kate were definitely going out.

Experienced former *The Sun* Royal reporter Paul Thompson rates it as one of the greatest exclusives of his career. 'Breaking the story that William and Kate were officially a couple was a massive scoop,' he said. 'I knew from a contact that Kate had been seen in Highgrove and that was very much key to the story. When the pictures appeared of them on the slopes together, it all made sense. It was always going to be a race between the papers to find out who William's first serious girlfriend was. I was confident that the story was right because of the quality of the information that I had.'

Paul, now working as a freelance reporter in the US, remembers too the furious reaction from William's press aides in the immediate aftermath. He said: 'Clarence House did get het up about the pictures, but banning Arthur was ridiculous. He hadn't even taken the photos that they were unhappy about! Eventually, after they had calmed down, they were prepared to admit off the record that the story was spot on. Of course, I never thought at that time that William and Kate would get married. They were young and it was way too early in their relationship to expect things would turn out like they have. But as it had transpired, he met the right girl at the right time.'

5

Rivals, Rows and the Real World

Just as Kate finally thought she had vanquished the competition, William threw a spanner into the works. He told her that he intended to jet to Africa for a summer break with Jecca, who was single after splitting from a long-term boyfriend. Kate's reaction to the planned trip isn't documented – but William cancelled it.

'This shows how seriously William is taking Kate,' one Royal insider said at the time. 'She did not put any pressure on him not to go to Africa, but he is a sensible person and knows how it would look. Spending time with an attractive girl he has been romantically linked with was not sensible.'

Instead, William and Kate took a break together with half a dozen other friends on the idyllic island of Rodrigues near Mauritius. But William also enjoyed a lads-only sailing holiday to Greece with six of his close buddies. Jecca – dressed in her trademark safari chic – was a guest at the wedding of Ed van Cutsem, William's close friend, for whom he was an usher. It was noticed by observers that she still moved in the same circles as William. And there were reports of a public row between William and Kate in his VW Golf outside a polo match in Coworth Park, Berkshire. Rumours of problems in the relationship were rife as the couple returned to St Andrews for their last academic

year together. As their finals hoved into view, they took stress-busting breaks to Balmoral and ski resort Verbier in Switzerland.

Despite frantically revising, Kate also found time to join William on his family holiday to Klosters for the second year running. It was to prove an extraordinarily eventful trip. Prince Charles, who was preparing to tie the knot with Camilla Parker Bowles the following week, was in a foul mood. He grimaced through an arranged photo opportunity with his sons – part of a deal with the media in return for being left alone for the rest of the break. But the entente cordiale descended into farce when he failed to realise that his mic was amplifying his whispered comments. The world's media heard every hushed word when he turned to his boys and slated the newsmen as 'these bloody people'.

Then, in a reference to respected BBC Royal correspondent Nicholas Witchell, he added: 'I can't bear that man. I mean, he's so awful, he really is.'

William was asked how he and Kate were coping with the attention. He batted the question away, saying: 'I haven't seen any of it. I'm just gagging to be on the slopes – simple as that.' Asked if there was likely to be a second Royal wedding soon, he simply said: 'No'.

Charles's blunder was, the press pack agreed, a belter of a story. But the night before those careless comments, *The Sun* Royal reporter Duncan Larcombe had landed an even better exclusive when William started opening up to him. When Duncan asked William if he was thinking of following in his father's footsteps by getting married, he laughed out loud. Then he blurted out: 'Look, I'm only 22 for God's sake. I am too young to marry at my age. I don't want to get married until I'm at least 28 or maybe 30.'

By the end of the night, Kate and William were in high spirits, running around the dance floor trying to pull down Guy Pelly's boxer shorts after the joker had stripped. Whether Kate was in such a good mood after reading William's views on marriage in the papers was unclear. But if there were any repercussions, William must have smoothed them over, for they were very much together as Graduation Day approached. Showing quite how much Kate was now part of The Firm — as the Royals are said to refer to themselves — Prince Charles invited her parents to dinner to mark the occasion. A family friend said: 'The Prince of Wales thinks the time has come for the two families to know each other a bit better.'

William Opens His Heart... to The Sun

Every national newspaper article about William and Kate's relationship always features the same key quote. It is from William, saying: 'I don't want to get married until I'm at least 28 or maybe 30.'

He came out with the famous line in a frank chat with Duncan Larcombe, then *The Sun's* Royal reporter, in the Casa Antica club, Klosters, in March 2005. Duncan remembers how the extraordinary night unfolded like it was yesterday. A number of other journalists had called it a night because of an early press call the next day, the one when Prince Charles infamously insulted BBC man Nicholas Witchell. Duncan went drinking instead with some of William's old friends from Eton.

He remembers: 'I was getting on well with them and they invited me to go on with them to the Casa Antica. The moment that we walked in, I spotted some of William and Harry's protection officers. I approached them to explain that I hadn't known that the princes would be there and volunteered to leave if they wanted me to. They were actually very relaxed and said that the boys were happy for me to come over and say "Hello". I knew Harry a little bit from previous trips and he introduced me to William. It was brief but friendly and I sat back down with the protection officers.'

At this point, fate – or Guy Pelly, to give him his full name – intervened. Duncan continues: 'From nowhere, Guy Pelly, who has always been the joker of the pack, jumped onto my lap wearing nothing but a pair of gold silk boxer shorts. One of the protection officers turned to him laughing and said, "Guy, have you met Duncan? He's *The Sun's* new Royal reporter…" In the second it took for the words to sink in, he leapt up and couldn't be seen for dust!

'William thought the whole thing was hilarious and came over to speak with me properly. He thanked the press for sticking to the St Andrews privacy pact, saying what an amazing time he'd had there. Then he asked me why there were so many photographers covering this trip – there must have been about 40 snappers on the slopes. He seemed genuinely baffled when I explained that there was huge interest because Kate could be his future wife. It was then that he said he wouldn't get married until he was 28 or maybe 30. I was so taken aback by what he had said that it was easy to recall it word for word.'

The quote has been used repeatedly ever since. But what did Duncan think the 22-year-old William really meant? He says: 'It always struck me as quite an odd thing to say. I never thought he was just kicking marriage into the long grass. One of the duties of an heir to the throne is to produce children for the line of succession. I always interpreted it to mean, "I know I'll have to marry young – but not this young."

It was the first non-staged interview with William and I think he knew exactly what he was doing. Both William and Harry are superb at managing their own public image whenever they are allowed to do so.'

William and Kate entered the graduation ceremony together looking very much a couple. Charles and Camilla both looked proud as
they looked on from the front row of the lower balcony in the university's Younger Hall. The Queen, who had not been feeling well, and
Prince Philip sat next to them. They were also naturally delighted to
see their grandson pick up his Master of Arts 2:1 degree in geography.
William, wearing a white bow tie and black academic gown, looked nervous and bit his lip. He was announced to the stage as 'William Wales'
and knelt before the chancellor as he received his scroll.

'I have thoroughly enjoyed my time at St Andrews and I shall be very sad to leave.'

Kate — wearing a short black skirt beneath her gown and high heels — sat five rows in front of her boyfriend and graduated 80 people ahead of him. She was called to the stage as 'Catherine Middleton' and grinned as she returned to her seat. Prince William kissed the Queen on both cheeks as she left and she patted his shoulder affectionately.

'Today is a very special day,' he said afterwards, 'and I am delighted that I can share it with my family, in particular with my grandmother, who has made such an effort to come, having been under the weather.' William himself was clearly sad at the prospect of leaving St Andrews after what had turned out — after an inauspicious start — to be a very happy four years. He praised the police for providing the extra security required by a long-term Royal stay and thanked the locals for their warm welcome. As many as 5,000 of them lined the streets to bid him a fond farewell — and to catch a final glimpse of Kate.

'I have thoroughly enjoyed my time at St Andrews and I shall be very sad to leave,' he said. 'I just want to say a big thank you to everyone who has made my time here so enjoyable. I'm going to miss Scotland — I have got used to the weather and all the golf chat.'

Dr Brian Lang, the vice-chancellor, offered prophetic words to the graduates as they prepared to launch themselves into the real world. He said: 'You will have made lifelong friends. I say this every year to all new graduates: you may have met your husband or wife.'

For Prince William and Kate Middleton, never had a truer word been spoken.

6

Soldier, Soldier

In the weeks before his graduation, William took steps that would map out his own future and have a crucial bearing on his relationship with Kate. He filled out an application for Army officer training at the Royal Military Academy in Sandhurst, Berkshire. Prince Harry seemed to be thriving on the world-renowned course having already enrolled after giving university a miss.

Just four months after William collected his geography degree, he too was accepted after passing the Regular Commissions Board selection process. 'I am absolutely delighted to have got over the first hurdle,' he said, 'but I am only too well aware, having spoken so much to Harry, that this is just the beginning. I am really looking forward to taking my place alongside all the other cadets at Sandhurst.'

His father and brother were both said to be 'absolutely thrilled' that William had signed up for military life. It was hardly a surprise. As future head of the Armed Forces, it was vital for him to get such experience under his belt.

Kate would have known of her boyfriend's plans but equally must have endured mixed feelings. The tough course, which would start the following January, lasted 44 weeks and would inevitably mean long

periods spent apart. Kate had witnessed how Harry's relationship with Chelsy Davy, his gorgeous Zimbabwean-born girlfriend, had struggled through the enforced separations of Army life. And if she had studied recent Royal history, she would have been well aware that the marriage of William's uncle Prince Andrew to Sarah Ferguson had suffered as a result of his commitments to the Royal Navy.

William also had plans to get a taste of work experience in other varied jobs before training started. These included land management on a farm and investment finance in the City. His final placement would be a stint as a trainee with RAF Valley's mountain rescue team in Anglesey, North Wales, which would prove to be a very influential spell when it came to his career choice years down the line.

But before the Army, the City or Valley, he seized the opportunity to take a last proper summer holiday. The rugby-mad Prince jetted to New Zealand to watch the ill-fated British and Irish Lions tour after an invitation from team manager Sir Clive Woodward. William didn't exactly prove to be a lucky charm as the visitors were thumped by a powerful All Blacks side in each of the three Tests.

But, as a foretaste of what his future life would hold, he under-took his first solo engagements representing the Queen. He took

part in two wreath-laying ceremonies to honour New Zealand soldiers who had died in war. And he visited a children's hospital in Auckland where his easy manner with sick kids drew inevitable comparisons with his mum. His down-to-earth charm during the whole tour — including sticking his thumbs up to a group of school-children — saw commentators pinpoint him as the future of the Royal Family.

With the official part of his holiday over, William flew on to Kenya to spend a month working at the Lewa Downs nature reserve owned by Jecca's parents. Kate was relaxed about the trip, a clear indication that she felt secure in their relationship. She showed that there were no bad feelings towards Jecca by joining her boyfriend on the break to sleep under the stars in a Masai hut. The Prince, Kate and seven pals had booked out all the £1,500-a-night lodges to celebrate graduating from university. Jecca shared a hut with her friends in a

lodge some yards away. She was now dating banker Hugh Crossley and enjoyed a 'brother–sister' relationship with William. As William and Kate watched rhino, zebra and antelope run free beneath the African sun, they enjoyed a rare moment of tranquillity.

If they ever paused to wonder where their relationship might be taking them, back home in Britain the bookies had no doubts. They were already offering odds of 3–1 against the couple tying the knot in 2008.

It was a low price that had been calculated with two momentous events in mind. Firstly, Prince Charles had given the green light to Kate spending nights at his son's apartment in Clarence House. Secondly, and perhaps even more significantly, she had been invited to dine with the Queen and Prince Philip for the first time.

Prince Charles and Camilla also attended what must have been a daunting evening in Balmoral for a young woman from the Home Counties. 'The Queen and Prince Philip think a lot of Kate,' a Royal insider explained. 'They admire the way she has conducted herself while being such a part of William's life over the last few years. The invitation to dinner is further evidence of the growing closeness and respect in which she is held.' Kate chalked up another coup when she met the Queen in Windsor Castle, the Monarch's favourite residence.

Her position as steady girlfriend to the future King was bizarrely confirmed publicly by a Williams – All Black forward Ali Williams – rather than a William.

The 6ft 7in giant spoke to the Prince about Kate at Buckingham Palace during a visit by the New Zealand side. He said afterwards of the conversation: 'He said it was going well, going steady. He seemed very content.' William and Kate spent Boxing Day at Sandringham, the Queen's Norfolk estate where Her Majesty traditionally gathers her family together for Christmas. They stayed in a cottage on Wolferton Marshes – a favourite remote spot for Royal shoots.

William whisked Kate off to Klosters just days before officer training was due to begin. As Army life loomed ever closer, the emotion of an imminent separation – William was banned from seeing friends and family for five weeks – bubbled to the surface. Despite having always previously kept a lid on their feelings in public, the couple leant in to kiss each other on the slopes of Casanna Alp. It was their first display of public passion captured on camera and *The Sun* was there to witness the moment on behalf of its readers.

The kiss was a visual rebuff to the naysayers who insisted their young love couldn't survive the threat of being apart. In another show of affection, William publicly referred to his girlfriend as 'my adorable Kate' at a surprise farewell party thrown in his honour.

The romantic Prince told friends and relatives that Kate would 'always' be in his thoughts.

THE FIRST KISS

The Sun photographer Scott Hornby took the first ever picture of William and Kate kissing.

The momentous event took place on the slopes of Casanna Alp in Klosters at the start of 2006. Scott says: 'I'd been out on the slopes for most of the day but pretty much given up catching sight of them. All of a sudden, they both came racing past me. William and Kate are both like Olympic skiers so there was no way I was even going to try to catch up with them.

'But I headed in their direction and half way down they stopped to take in the great view of the mountains. I almost went past them, but whipped out my camera from my backpack and took a shot on the move. And as good fortune would have it, they were kissing. It was a lucky day.'

He stuck by her side at the Clarence House champagne bash, which was followed by a reception at a Mayfair restaurant and a nightclub. And then it was time for William to start a new chapter in his life.

On arrival at Sandhurst, kisses with Kate and glasses of bubbly must have seemed like a dim and distant dream. Although he knew that the training would be hardcore, Officer Cadet Wales — as William would be known — managed to raise a smile.

He joked that he had put Harry in first as a 'guinea pig'. William also endured the gnawing fear that an Army grade-two razor haircut would expose his thinning hair. In an interview given while he was still at St Andrews, he spelt out that he would never want special treatment if he were to join up. 'The last thing I want is to be mollycoddled or wrapped up in cotton wool,' he said, 'because, if I was to join the Army, I'd want to go where my men went and I'd want to do what they did. It's the most humiliating thing, and it would be something I'd find very awkward to live with, being told I couldn't go out there when these guys have got to go out there and do a bad job.'

The imposing figure of Major General Andrew Ritchie, the Academy's commandant, assured reporters that William shouldn't lose any sleep about soft-soap treatment. 'Although Prince William is the future head of the Armed Forces, he will be treated the same as every other cadet,' he said. After a couple of weeks' training, William would no doubt have bitten off the senior officer's hand for a bit of mollycoddling. The gruelling regime included 18-hour days that started with the unmistakeable bashing together of dustbin lids at dawn, after an uncomfortable night spent without a quilt.

As part of Blenheim Company, William learnt leadership and general soldiering. In stark contrast to a life spent growing up in palaces, he polished his own boots and ironed his own trousers. Like the other 269 Sandhurst cadets enrolling with him, he had brought his own ironing board with him when Prince Charles dropped him off.

After dozing through his 5.30 am alarm on a string of mornings, he took to sleeping on the floor. It was an extreme measure, but one that meant that he was ready for inspection immediately without having to make his bed. He placed a picture of Kate in his room next to one of his parents in happier times. The old-fashioned Royal tried to ease the pain of separation by sending Kate handwritten, heartfelt, love notes.

He sweetly addressed her by the pet name 'Babykins', while her letters jokingly referred to him as 'Big Willie'. In a more practical display of devotion, William also made certain that Kate's £800,000 Chelsea flat was kitted out with a state-of-the-art security system. He had been left spitting with rage after a German newspaper printed photographs of the property that pinpointed its exact location.

After William completed the five-week basic training, he and Kate spent part of their first weekend together relaxing at the Tunnel House Inn in Cirencester, Gloucestershire. Now that the ban from seeing friends was lifted, William regularly drove the 45 minutes from his barracks to Kate's family home for evenings together. He could relax with the Middletons and even took his turn doing the washing up. And he proudly showed Kate around the base when she visited with Prince Charles in February.

' William regularly drove the 45 minutes from his barracks to Kate's family home for evenings together.'

The Prince of Wales and his future daughter-in-law joined William for a curry lunch with other members of his company in Old College. 'They seemed besotted with each other,' said a military source who witnessed the meal.

Kate needed to fashion a social life in William's absence but still maintained her Royal links. She made a surprise appearance with Charles and Camilla — but not William, who was confined to his barracks — at the Cheltenham Gold Cup. Kate was chaperoned by Thomas van Straubenzee, her boyfriend's closest chum.

William was spending his days dressed in camouflage and combat fatigues for training that included learning how to fire an SA80 rifle. The time away from Kate gave him perspective and brought the relationship into focus for him. The pair were snapped gazing into each other's eyes outside a nightclub during his four weeks off from Sandhurst in the summer. 'William has spent as much time as possible with Kate during the break, which is very telling,' a Royal source said at the time. 'All that time spent training in the cold and damp, sitting in ditches and the like, have made William realise what is important.' As he approached his passing-out date, he joined his fellow cadets for a ten-day exercise in Cyprus — another spell away from his girlfriend.

When, against all expectation, Kate made her grand entrance at the parade in December, it was clear just quite how much she meant to William. It was her debut appearance at an official Royal engagement and represented the first formal confirmation that the couple were an item. Observers recalled that Chelsy had not been invited to Harry's passing out at Sandhurst earlier in the same year. Kate, who was joined by her mum and dad, looked a vision in a striking bright-red winter coat and black broad-brimmed hat. For the group of photographers shivering on a freezing winter's day, it was a sight to warm the heart. Their shutters clacked like machine gun fire as Kate braved a bitter wind along Sandhurst's King's Walk to take a seat in the stand.

Kate was accompanied by Jamie Lowther-Pinkerton, the former SAS officer who had been appointed William's private secretary. Moments later, Charles and Camilla walked through the same entrance, followed by the Queen and Prince Philip. All of them wore proud expressions as William — alongside 500 fellow cadets — took part in the Sovereign's Parade to become an Army officer. At one point during the ceremony, a lip-reader hired by a TV station spotted Kate saying: 'I love the uniform. So, so sexy.'

Royal sources described her attendance as 'significant', saying: 'Everyone knows they are a serious item, but this is, if you like, the first time they have allowed it to be put on public display.'

William wore a red sash to identify him as an escort of the Sovereign's Banner, the prize his platoon had won during training. He became 2nd Lieutenant Wales as he received his Army commission and would join the Household Cavalry's Blues and Royals.

William and his fellow new officers were given the honour of being inspected by the Queen. Her Majesty paused in front of her grandson to utter a few words – audible only to them – that made him smile. But she wasn't asking him the one question on everyone else's lips: 'When are you going to marry that girl?'

'Her Majesty paused in front of William to utter a few words—audible only to them—that made him smile.'

7

Work Hard, Play Hard

On the rare occasions in 2006 that William wasn't knee deep in mud on exercise, he and Kate indulged their twin passions: clubbing and foreign travel. Like any young couple fresh from university, they wanted to enjoy their freedom from years in the academic pressure cooker by letting off steam. William, of course, still had the responsibilities and workload of Sandhurst to contend with. But whenever he had a night off or a break from training, he would spend it having fun with Kate.

London remains the best city in the world for night life and being a Prince - or a Prince's girlfriend - meant guaranteed entry to all of the coolest venues. Exotically named establishments like Mahiki, Boujis, Embassy and Whisky Mist became as familiar to Royal watchers as Highgrove, Sandringham and Balmoral. Here, William and Kate would party with a close-knit group of friends, drinking potent cocktails and dancing into the small hours.

King Of Clubs (& Restaurants)

If you want to live like a King – or a future King at least – or the evening, start off for dinner in Chelsea.

William and Kate enjoy eating in a variety of London restaurants… as long as they have an SW3 or SW10 postcode. You could pretty much stick a pin in a map of the area and it would land on an eaterie they have frequented. Favourites include the Bluebird, Tom Aikens, La Famiglia, Gilmour's, or the Pig's Ear gastropub. The couple have gone off piste on the odd occasion – once heading for Dans Le Noir? in Clerkenwell, where diners eat in the pitch black.

After letting dinner go down, the next stop is a cocktail at Raffles – appropriately enough on nearby King's Road – followed by a gin and tonic at Kitts on Sloane Square. From there, it's a taxi into Mayfair to the night-clubs that provided the backdrop for much of William and Kate's courtship. Head to Mahiki on Dover Street to take on the £100 Treasure Chest cock-tail. If you're still standing, it's on to Whisky Mist inside the Park Lane Hilton. And if you've got any cash left after that, you might want to book a room.

Harry's passing out at Sandhurst in April fired the starting pistol for one of William's more controversial nights on the tiles. It began with a formal ball at the military academy, where a flowing free bar ensured spirits were high.

William - who had just started a month-long break from training - laughed uproariously at some near-the-knuckle jokes being told by his pals. Top brass would later complain to Clarence House about the raucous behaviour of his group. Harry spent his time glued to Chelsy, who had joined him for the evening celebration and looked gorgeous in a turquoise silk gown. William left the ball early but carried on drinking through the night in his barracks. The very next evening, the princes and their girlfriends carried on partying at Boujis, shelling out a reported £2,500 on champagne and cocktails. Ever-sensible Kate was the first to leave just before 2 am, followed by Harry 40 minutes later. William and Chelsy emerged together, bleary eyed, at 3.30 am.

William recovered in time to jet off to the Caribbean for a £30,000 Easter sunshine break with Kate - their first trip away together since he had entered Sandhurst. They were joined in Mustique by other friends from home and whiled away blissful hours playing volleyball and Frisbee. John and Belle Robinson - owners of high street fashion store Jigsaw - lent the group Villa Hibiscus, their £8,000-a-week holiday home. The five-bedroom hilltop property was, as luck would have it, fit for a King. It boasted an infinity pool with views of a white sand beach.

Kate showed off her trim figure in a white and turquoise bikini as she soaked up the 30°C sunshine on a leisurely cruise around the coast in a luxury motor boat. William sported a pair of red shorts and was clearly revelling in the physique his Army training had given him. He couldn't resist showing off by doing his best Tarzan impression as he swung from a cable on the vessel. Evenings were spent at Basil's Bar - a favourite of Princess Margaret, William's great-aunt - where the Prince and his pals belted out Elvis classics on the karaoke machine. The holiday seemed to end as quickly as it had begun, as the couple had to return in time for the society wedding of Camilla's daughter Laura Parker Bowles to Harry Lopes in Wiltshire.

But William's summer break handed them another chance to get away, and this time they plumped for Ibiza, something of an unusual destination for the Royals. They stayed with Kate's uncle, Gary Goldsmith - mum Carole's brother - in his £5-million villa. Uncle Gary and his white-walled property, which was bizarrely called La Maison de Bang Bang, would come back to haunt William and Kate. They enjoyed a chartered boat trip around the Balearic rave island and even treated themselves to a mud bath at a spa.

After returning from the trip, they squeezed in a last night at Boujis before William returned to Sandhurst. It was the night that their adoring look in the back seat of a Range Rover as they left at 3.30 am was caught by photographers. The clubs and holidays were clearly more than adequate compensation for the time apart.

But while the relationship seemed to have ridden out the difficulties of military life, Kate was facing other awkward questions. What, some unfriendly voices in the media demanded to know, was she planning to do for a living?

More than a year after graduating, she didn't appear to have a job. Rumours that she planned to launch a range of children's wear had come to nothing. In November, however, all that changed as she was hired by Jigsaw – whose owners, the Robinsons, had lent her and William the villa in Mustique.

She would spend four days a week working as an accessories buyer at the head office of the fashion firm in Kew, West London. She immediately got stuck into her new role and proved that she did not expect special treatment by making cups of tea for everyone during a fashion shoot. 'There is nothing snooty about Kate,' said a worker at the session.

'She was determined to make herself useful during the shoot - and that included making tea.' He added: 'Some of the staff there did find it a bit odd being waited on by the potential future Queen. But it shows William has pulled a real cracker with no airs and graces. He's a lucky chap.'

'More than a year after graduating,' she didn't appear to have a job.'

All looked rosy. Kate was working, William was about to finish Sandhurst and the relationship was flourishing. High street store Woolworths became so convinced of an impending engagement that it started work on wedding souvenirs. (As it transpired, William and Kate would outlast the ailing retailer, which went bust in the recession two years later.) Kate was well liked at Jigsaw and her new friends seized on the reports about the cheesy gifts. One bought her a homemade mug for Christmas featuring a snap of her and William together in an ironic nod to the Woolworths line. Everyone roared with laughter, no one more so than the victim of the cheeky joke.

Days before Christmas, Kate showed that her daring streak - last seen at the St Andrews fashion show all those years ago - hadn't quite deserted her. She donned a pair of fishnet tights beneath a black dress as she and William joined Harry for a night's partying at the Embassy Club in Mayfair.

200?

CELEBRATING THE ROYAL MARRIAGE
OF
William & Kate
MONTH DATE 2007

Kate spent that Christmas with her family in a Scottish manor house, contrary to unfounded rumours that the Queen had invited her to Sandringham.

As the New Year arrived, speculation that William was about to pop the question reached fever pitch. Kate's soaring public profile attracted the attention of a pack of paparazzi photographers. Police were called by William's personal protection officers to provide an escort as she left Boujis at 3 am. They feared that the situation would get out of hand if reinforcements weren't brought in.

Kate faced the same lenses every morning as she left her flat and climbed into her VW Golf to drive to work. Four officers were placed outside the property to keep a close eye on developments. The situation was especially sensitive to William, who was said to be 'very angry' and 'enormously frustrated' by what he saw as harassment. To make matters worse, it came in the wake

vate
perty -
arking

of Lord Stevens's report into his mother's death and just before a new inquest into it was due to open. Things came to a head in the week William reported for duty with his new regiment, the Blues and Royals, at Combermere Barracks in Windsor, Berkshire.

A pack of around 50 photographers and cameramen waited for Kate to leave her flat on 9 January, the day of her 25th birthday. Kate tried not to react to the mêlée, but was clearly unhappy. *The Sun* announced that it would not publish paparazzi shots of her.

The only bright spot for her was that the £40 black-and-white Topshop dress she was wearing sold out in less than a week.

Many were convinced it wouldn't be long before the dress captivating

the public would be a white one. The couple's body language in an Alpine restaurant on their first holiday of 2007 suggested as much. William held Kate in his arms, embraced her for more than a minute and planted a tender kiss on her cheek. A diner who saw the display of affection in Zermatt, Switzerland, said: 'They were so happy together. It's obvious they have that special chemistry. There were at least 70 other people having lunch but William seemed happy to show her affection in front of everyone. Throughout lunch Kate gazed at William and had a permanent smile fixed across her face.'

Everything, it seemed, pointed to a wedding. Until, that was, the unthinkable happened.

8

Splitting Up ... and Getting Back Together

Fashion editors were agreed that Cheltenham 2007 was not William and Kate's finest hour. They had arrived at the popular horse racing festival wearing matching tweed. Their outfits, it was said, were more suited to Charles and Camilla. They looked uncomfortable, a far cry from the tactile young couple who had held each other on the slopes just weeks earlier. William was about to leave for Bovington Camp in Dorset where he would learn how to command tanks.

Suddenly, seemingly out of nowhere, cracks started appearing in the relationship.

William spent a night dancing on a podium with blonde 19-year-old Lisa Agar at Elements nightclub in Bournemouth. He had been downing pints of Stella Artois and shots of sambuca with fellow officers from the Household Cavalry on their first night off from the course. Lisa joined him at the officers' mess, stayed until 4.15 am and afterwards claimed the future King had been pretty drunk.

'He was very affectionate and touchy-feely,' she said. 'And he definitely wasn't a shy boy.' Then, in words that must have stung Kate like salt in a wound, she went on:

'But not once did he talk about Kate. It was as though she didn't exist. I spent almost the whole time at the club with him - we drank, we danced, we went back to his place.'

Lisa admitted that nothing untoward had happened between her and the Prince. Relaxed Clarence House aides laughed off the

incident as a storm in a shot glass. But then *The Sun* published photos of William grabbing 18-year-old Brazilian student Ana Ferreira's boob. Confessing that she was drunk herself, she said: 'I felt something brush my breast. I thought it couldn't be the future King - but now I've seen the picture it's no wonder he has a smile on his face! He has big manly hands and certainly knows what to do with them.' William, it was universally agreed, had some serious grovelling in store when he next saw Kate.

But despite these indiscretions, no one saw what was coming next. The world was left stunned by *The Sun* man Duncan Larcombe's exclusive scoop on 14 April 2007: 'Wills and Kate split'.

The separation was amicable, he wrote, but their relationship had suffered since he had left Sandhurst. By putting his military career first, William had placed it under intolerable pressure. He preferred to go drinking with his Army pals rather than drive from Bovington to Chelsea or Bucklebury to see his girlfriend.

'As far as Kate is concerned, William simply hasn't been paying her enough attention,' said one close friend of the couple. 'She is stuck in London while he is living in an officer's mess in Dorset. Kate feels hugely frustrated that their relationship just seems to be going backwards at a rate of knots. At university they were living together. Now, nearly three years on, they are lucky if they see each other once a week. When he does get a night off, it appears to Kate that William would rather spend time drinking with his new-found Army pals.'

Breaking the Break Up

William and Kate's split in April 2007 was another world exclusive broken by *The Sun*'s Duncan Larcombe.

He says: 'It was completely unexpected because everything seemed so rosy. William had been partying with other officers at clubs near Bovington Camp rather than spending time with Kate. I think Kate's the kind of girl who shows complete loyalty in a relationship and expects the same in return. I think there had been other problems and seeing him pictured in the papers with other women was the final straw. She warned him that he either treated her properly or he could forget the whole thing.'

The paper knew that it had a 'super-belter' of a story on its hands. Instead of publishing it in the first two editions, we spoofed – industry jargon for using a different front page in early print runs to stop rivals lifting the real story.

Duncan, now *The Sun*'s Defence Editor, says: 'No one else got a sniff of it, which was fantastic. Obviously I can't reveal exactly who gave me the story, but I can say that it was someone with links to Kate rather than William. I think they felt she was being treated pretty poorly and wanted her side to come out. My abiding memory of the aftermath was that everyone was amazed by the turn of events.

'I saw someone close to William a couple of weeks later and he said: "Those two, eh? Who knew that would happen?" I think in the long run it made the relationship stronger. Once they got back together, William would never mess about in any capacity with other women, however innocent. There was never any doubt after their reunion that they would get married.'

WILLS' OLD RIVAL DATES KATE

By CLODAGH HARTLEY

PRINCE William's ex Kate Middleton has a new date — one of his former love rivals.

Shipping heir Henry Ropner, 25, used to go out with Jecca Craig — and when they split in 2003, Wills stepped in.

Now Kate, 25 — whose relationship with the prince ended in April — has been "enjoying Henry's company" on regular nights out in London.

Full Story — Page Four

Out . . . Henry and Kate this week

Kate was said to be livid that William's pals Guy Pelly and Thomas van Straubanzee had been invited along to Zermatt on their skiing holiday. And there were snide claims that Kate's mum Carole had not been posh enough to cut it with the Palace - something always strenuously denied by Clarence House sources. It was rumoured that a circle of William's friends would whisper 'doors to manual' when Kate approached, a snobbish reference to Carole's past as an air hostess.

Royal sources say neither William nor Kate believe the jibe was ever uttered. The night before the news broke, William partied with eight friends at Mahiki. He suggested to his chums that they drink their way through the bar's menu and was seen with its signature £100 Treasure Chest cocktail at his table. Before long, he was on the dancefloor singing along to the Rolling Stones' anthem 'You Can't Always Get What You Want'.

Brave Kate refused to retreat into her shell. Instead, she dressed up and partied like never before. She showed off her figure in a 1970s-style dress and boots as she hit Mahiki with her own friends.

She was seen laughing and drinking champagne with William's chum James Meade in the VIP stand at the Badminton Horse Trials in Gloucestershire. Socialites including Tara Palmer-Tomkinson flocked round her during a heavyweight book launch at Asprey jewellers in London. Two weeks after the split became public, she danced at Mahiki and Boujis on the same night with a trio of male friends from William's circle. Glasses Direct millionaire Jamie Murray Wells and estate agent Charlie Morshead were both eligible bachelors.

'A friend of the couple said: "William invited Kate to Clarence House to smooth things over...He made it obvious that he hasn't got over her."'

Old Etonian shipping heir Henry Ropner had a girlfriend but in the past had dated Jecca. And she jetted off to Ibiza for a break with pal Emilia D'Erlanger - herself once linked to Wills - and other friends, including her brother James.

Then just as suddenly as they split, the fairytale romance seemed to be dramatically back on.

In June, Kate appeared with William at a Moulin Rouge-themed Army fancy dress party in Bovington. Sharp-eyed guests were transfixed at they spotted the pair - neither of whom had gone for outlandish outfits - kissing on the dancefloor. Moments later, the couple made a beeline for Williams's quarters. It was the preamble to an emotional

showdown in which William begged Kate to take him back.

A friend of the couple said: 'William invited Kate to Clarence House to smooth things over. They had a first awkward drink but then talked about their split. He made it obvious that he hasn't got over her. Kate is in the driving seat.'

She did, however, accept his invitation to the Concert for Diana

at Wembley Stadium, held in memory of William's mum. The night before the gig, Kate parked her Audi A3 in a hotel car park near Clarence House and sneaked in shortly after midnight.

A flunky was despatched a couple of hours later to drive the car into the Royal residence. She sat in the row behind him at the concert and danced to the likes of Lily Allen, Take That and Kanye West. Later

at the after show party, she drank cocktails and shared another dance with William. They had definitely kissed and made up.

Shortly afterwards, William showed that Kate was completely back into the fold by bringing her to Camilla's 60th birthday party at Highgrove. She wore a full-length cream dress and smooched with William to Frank Sinatra's 'It Had to Be You'.

Kate pulled out of a charity attempt to cross the Channel in a dragon boat with 16 other girls. This was interpreted as a sign that she was being advised by Clarence House aides, who did not want her to invite the attention of the paparazzi.

Then the holidays began again. Kate and William flew to isolated Desroches Island in the Seychelles to seal their reunion. And they showed their sense of humour by checking in to the £5,000-a-week resort using the aliases Martin and Rose Middleton. It was a game William had learnt from Prince Charles, who jokingly referred to himself and Camilla as Fred and Gladys.

Back in London, they were spotted out together for the first time since the split leaving Boujis - where else? If there was any lingering doubt over the state of the relationship, the answer lay, as ever, with the bookies. They had stopped taking bets that William and Kate would tie the knot.

9

The Waiting Game

After the emotional upheaval of splitting up and getting back together, William and Kate were back on an even keel. They flew to Balmoral to spend time with Charles and Camilla, where Kate caused some controversy by donning camouflage gear to stalk deer on the estate. She would show similar dedication to her boyfriend by collecting dead pheasants for him on a shoot in Windsor Great Park. As Christmas approached, the couple delighted ice skaters at Somerset House in London by gliding around the outdoor rink. The next few months

were spent making career decisions that would define the next period of their relationship.

William reached another milestone in the Army when he passed his tank commander course. He now embarked on a bespoke arrangement to give him a taste of the Air Force and the Navy. At the start of 2008, he began a four-month secondment from the Blues and Royals to RAF Cranwell in Lincolnshire.

Kate clapped proudly when William received his provisional Wings from Prince Charles at Cranwell at the end of the 12-week course. She looked radiant in a cream double-breasted coat and black boots at her second official engagement as William's girlfriend. Flying Officer William Wales — as he was now known in the RAF — was also supported by Camilla and his aunt Lady Sarah McCorquodale, Diana's sister. Tellingly, Kate seemed entirely assured of her status and appeared at home mingling in Royal company.

William had clearly excelled on his tailor-made short course flying fast propeller-powered planes and helicopters. Wing Commander Andy Lovell, who helped train the young Prince, hailed him as a quick learner. 'I was impressed by his flying skills,' he said. It soon emerged that William enjoyed flying so much that he had cheekily undertaken five 'special' sorties costing £86,000. Unable to resist showing off his new-found skills, he had landed an RAF Chinook in a field near Kate's family home.

He had also flown to the Isle of Wight for cousin Peter Phillips's stag do, a wedding bash in Hexham, Northumberland, and over Royal residences Highgrove and Sandringham. William's instructors insisted they had used the properties as markers to plot flight courses. But the furious Chief of the Air Staff, Air Chief Marshall Sir Glen Torpy, was said to have 'flipped a track' at the excursions.

While William was on the back foot as he waited for the flights furore to subside, Kate too was facing flak. Weeks before William had started at Cranwell, she quit her job at Jigsaw after just a year. The move inevitably sparked another frenzy of engagement

speculation. But it also triggered an unprecedented wave of criticism against her. She faced accusations that she was work-shy and only waiting for William to put a ring on her finger. Detractors claimed that some of her circle had cruelly started referring to her as 'Waity Katy'. Those close to William say the couple have dismissed the nickname as a media invention.

Kate took a job with the family business but again her enemies derided it as an easy option. Clarence House sources have defended her career choices to the hilt. 'Kate was well liked at Jigsaw and

worked incredibly hard,' said one aide close to William. 'It was the situation with photographers gathering outside her flat that made it impossible for her to continue with a job in London. It wasn't just Jigsaw, it pretty much ruled out any job in the capital. The job with Party Pieces isn't some sort of cop out, as it's sometimes unfairly portrayed. She's been involved in marketing products for the firm and heads up a team. And she works bloody long hours as you would expect in a successful family business.'

Kate held her head high and ignored the jibes. She represented William at Peter Phillips's wedding, while the Prince flew to Kenya to watch ex-sweetheart Jecca Craig's brother Batian tie the knot with Melissa Duveen.

Peter's nuptials became embroiled in controversy after he and his fiancée Autumn Kelly struck a £500,000 deal with *Hello!* magazine. But Kate and Chelsy, who was also there, were praised for not stealing the bride's glory by staying out of the limelight. Kate spent more time with pals at social bashes, including the Nelson Mandela 90th birthday gig in Hyde Park and the tennis at Wimbledon. Despite the hard time she was getting from some of the media, she managed to retain her sense of humour.

She stifled giggles as William was installed as a Knight of the Garter. She even blurted out 'Oh my God!' as she caught sight of her boyfriend in the full regalia, which included an ostrich feather hat.

'Kate took a job with the family business but again her enemies derided it as an easy option.'

In summer 2008, William joined the Navy for a two-month detachment as Sub-Lieutenant William Wales. He served for five weeks on the Type 23 frigate HMS Iron Duke battling cocaine trafficking in the Caribbean and was praised for his part in a dramatic £40-million drugs bust on the high seas. The Prince was a lookout on a Navy Lynx chopper that swooped on a suspicious powerboat north-east of Barbados. Once again, William and Kate could only stay in contact by writing letters but they were now at least used to the time apart. At the end of July, Kate jetted to Mustique for a romantic rendezvous with William after he left the ship. Showing a canny awareness of public perceptions, she refused an upgrade to first class on the flight out.

If she wasn't already switched on to the pitfalls of life as a Royal girlfriend, a plot by thieves to sell stolen pictures of her and William would have served as a reminder.

The Sun was offered private snaps of the couple in Mustique for £50,000 after a camera belonging to Kate's younger sister Pippa was nicked.

Among the 40 photos were images of Kate doing yoga in a bikini, and William relaxing with his girlfriend and her family. We tipped off the police. Market trader Charlie Ewins and electrician Leon Sesay later admitted to stealing the camera's flashcard. Recorder Martyn Barklem later sentenced them to 100 hours community service after praising *The Sun* for shopping the pair. 'You approached *The Sun* newspaper,' he said,

'and to its credit that resulted in the police being notified and the card being returned to the owner and the images not splashed around the world. Had you gone to some foreign news agency the consequences could have been different.' He added: 'I suppose years ago you might have been sent to the Tower of London but of course cameras and memory cards did not exist in those days.'

William was naturally angry about the episode but he also had other things on his mind. He had just made a decision about his future that would wrongfoot everyone.

'She managed to retain her sense of humour. She stifled giggles as William was installed as a Knight of the Garter.'

10

The Pilot Prince

William was widely expected to leave the military after finishing his stint with the Navy. He could now become head of the Armed Forces safe in the knowledge that he had experience of the three services. All indications were that he was preparing to shoulder the burden of duty as a full-time working member of the Royal Family.

It was also considered a given that an engagement announcement would follow in due course.

William, however, is considered stubborn by even some of his closest friends. He had no plans to be bounced into anything he didn't feel ready for, whether it be Royal service or marriage. So in September 2008, it was announced that the second-in-line to the throne would train to become a full-time RAF search-and-rescue pilot. 'The time I spent with the RAF earlier this year made me realise how much I love flying,' he said. 'Joining search and rescue is a perfect opportunity for me to serve in the Forces operationally.'

The training and a three-year tour of duty meant William was committed to life in the RAF until summer 2013. But he had talked things through with Kate and it was an excellent decision. It presented him with an opportunity to play a meaningful role without ever having to face a war zone. Prince Harry had already spent 10

weeks working as a forward air controller in Afghanistan's Helmand Province from the end of 2007.

William had been envious of his brother's heroics, even though he knew in his heart of hearts it was almost certain he could never follow suit. 'I'd love to do what Harry did out in Afghanistan,' he reportedly told a clubber in Whisky Mist. 'That's why we train, because we want to be out there on the front line. I'm a bit jealous of him to be honest. Hopefully I'll get my turn.' Search and rescue offered an element of risk that was acceptable to the suited advisers who had a big say in his future. Even though search-and-rescue teams could be sent to Afghanistan, saving stranded climbers and trawlermen was a more likely scenario.

Although Kate knew that she faced more time apart from William, she was happy that she remained an integral part of his plans. This was amply demonstrated when she and Chelsy were invited to their first formal Buckingham Palace reception for Prince Charles's 60th birthday. Stars from the world of entertainment including Stephen Fry, Joanna Lumley and Rowan Atkinson lit up the Clarence House bash. But Kate wasn't fazed by celebrities or Royals, and danced with William as Scots rocker Rod Stewart belted out some of his classics.

She was also finding — and occasionally losing — her own feet in the charity world as she organised a roller disco. She wore a sequinned turquoise halterneck, yellow hotpants and knee-length electric pink socks for the midnight party.

Kate and pal Holly Branson — daughter of Virgin tycoon Sir Richard — had launched it in honour of Kate's boarding-school pal Thomas Waley-Cohen. He had died of bone cancer aged 20 in 2004 and money from the event would go towards raising £100,000 for a surgical ward at Oxford Children's Hospital.

William also found himself on wheels as his insatiable appetite for adventure took him to Africa for a motorbike trek with Harry. The eight-day off-road ride with Prince Harry spanned 1,000 miles across South Africa and Lesotho in temperatures of 40°C.

Back in Britain, Kate and William celebrated approaching their sixth Christmas together by joining Harry for a pheasant shoot in Sandringham. William was sporting a beard that he grew while on a 10 day exercise with the Special Boat Service.

' Although Kate knew that she faced more time apart from William, she was happy that she remained an integral part of his plans.'

He stayed in Sandringham for the festive period while Kate enjoyed a family holiday in Mustique. They spent New Year at Prince Charles's private retreat Birkhall on the Queen's Balmoral estate with Charles and Camilla. Romantic William surprised Kate with a candlelit dinner in a secluded log cabin decked out with a crisp linen tablecloth and silver cutlery. The pair returned to London — by which time William had shaved off his beard — and spent Kate's birthday together.

William's flying training began in earnest at RAF Shawbury in Shropshire.

He rented a stone cottage nearby to which Kate became a regular visitor. It wasn't exactly a lovers' retreat though – Prince Harry was also at the base for Army Air Corps training and moved in to share digs.

Soon after William's training began, he joined Kate and her family for a ski trip in Courchevel. Aware of the global recession biting into his future subjects, he sat in economy for the flight out.

When he was next seen with Kate, at an Ascot polo match – despite the fact she suffers an allergy to horses – it had been five months since they were last spotted together. The couple enjoyed a carefree long weekend away in Cornwall, booking themselves into a hotel as Mr and Mrs Smith. They were joined by Harry and friends for a relaxing couple of days playing tennis and tucked into barbecue grub on the beach. Kate took another break to Mustique, but it was a link to a different holiday that was suddenly causing headaches.

Her uncle Gary Goldsmith, whom she and William had stayed with in Ibiza in 2006, had embarrassingly bragged to undercover journalists that he had once greeted William with the line: 'Oi, you f***er!'

He claimed that he had sworn at the future King after William broke some ornamental glass pyramids while throwing balls around his La Maison de Bang Bang villa.

The black sheep of the Middleton family, Goldsmith made his fortune in IT recruitment and was said to have the words 'Nouveau Riche' tattooed across his shoulders.

He suggested that William had once made a crude joke about Kate's boobs at the Middleton family dinner table. And he remembered that friends had been teaching the Prince how to mix records on DJ decks. 'Yeah, it was brilliant,' he said. 'And they told him he needs a shout, "The King's in da house!" He's a very friendly guy.' He also jokingly suggested that he would be giving Kate away at her wedding.

The story clearly didn't affect William's love for Kate – they were pictured kissing in a country pub the day after it was published. And when they arrived at the wedding of William's chum Nicholas van Cutsem to Alice Hadden-Paton, the groom joked: 'You'll be next!'

Having spent a month at RAF Valley in Anglesey improving his flying skills, William and Kate took off to one of their favourite destinations – Mustique. On their return, Kate hosted a table at a bash held in London's Saatchi Gallery for the Starlight Children's Foundation, a charity she supports.

She was praised for her demeanour in a role she will no doubt
be expected to carry out regularly in the future. William showed
his own charitable side when he and Harry backed *The Sun's* second
Military Awards in December. The young princes were the stars
of the show, mixing as easily with like-minded servicemen and
women as they did with showbiz stars.

William also showed his dedication to Centrepoint, the charity
for young homeless people of which he is patron, by spending a
night sleeping rough in London. As 2009 approached its end,
the Queen issued a blunt warning to paparazzi photographers that
the private lives of the Royals must not be breached. It was seen,
inevitably, as a cue for a pending engagement announcement.

WILLIAM & KATE

181

THE ROYAL LOVE STORY

11

Wait and See

William spent the start of 2010 on his first official foreign tour in New Zealand and Australia. The trip was considered a great success, with enormous crowds lining the streets for every engagement. In Wellington, thousands waited for him as he opened the new Supreme Court building as the Queen's representative. Even in Sydney and Melbourne – modern cities considered to hold republican sympathies – the turnout was huge. As Kate still did not have a ring on her finger, she did not accompany William on the tour.

Every single time William came into contact with the crowds, the same question would rise above the general hubbub. 'William, when are you going to marry Kate?' a wag would yell, obviously believing it to be the first time anyone had thought to ask.

Despite the scorching southern hemisphere heat and a packed schedule, William bore the repeated inquiries with Zen-like good grace. Every time his reply was the same: 'Wait and see. Just wait and see.' He even took it in good spirits when, on a trip to Eden Park Stadium in Auckland, schoolboy Sebastian Diedricks hurled a rugby ball into his groin. The cheeky ten-year-old later apologised… to Kate.

The day before flying to New Zealand, William had received a certificate confirming that he had attained his 'proper' provisional RAF wings. He got them for completing the full 12-month flying course, rather than the specially adapted course he had taken at RAF Cranwell two years earlier. William's father presented him with the honour at a ceremony attended by Kate in RAF Shawbury. Prince Charles made reference to how difficult life was for the girlfriends of those in his son's line of work. 'I know only too well how complicated it can be having a relative or a close friend in the forces, because they are rarely, if ever, around,' he said. 'But today is a day, I think, of great pride for all of the parents, not to mention the girlfriends. We all know how hard our sons have worked in between all the other activities that we don't know about.' Proud Kate gave William a standing ovation for his efforts and he arranged for her to take a fun flight in a Griffin chopper.

On his return from Down Under, William began the next stage of his RAF career – learning how to fly the iconic yellow Sea King rescue helicopter. After an initial stint at ground school at Royal Naval Air Station in Culdrose, Cornwall, he returned again to RAF Valley. It was, of course, the same base where he had been on mountain rescue work experience after university. He was expected to stay there until September, when he would be posted for his three-year operational tour. Unbeknown to Kate – or indeed to William at that stage – Valley was set to be his home for the next four years.

'Proud Kate gave William a standing ovation for his efforts and he arranged for her to take a fun flight in a Griffin chopper.'

William decided that he liked the isolated location and listed it as one of his two preferred bases for the tour. Top brass agreed that it fitted in with their operational requirements, meaning North Wales would be William's stomping ground until September 2013.

The couple wasted no time in picking out a scenic cottage to give them a cosy place to live – and some privacy.

William's career, the cottage and Anglesey's location all give Kate time to get used to one day becoming Queen.

Life as a serviceman's wife may not be as thrilling as the clubs and parties of London but it will give her a solid foundation at the start of the marriage. It will certainly be a calmer introduction to Royal life than that faced by Princess Diana, who had just turned 20 when she married Charles.

From speaking to William about his trip to New Zealand and Australia, she has a good idea of what the coming years hold. It is a future in which she will accompany him around the world as they represent their country and its subjects. It is one that will require a good nature, patience, hard work, resolve, tact and diplomacy. She will undoubtedly need William's support and, most importantly, his love.

But those who have watched the couple develop over their years together have no doubts that the Monarchy is in safe hands.

Where Will They Honeymoon?

The Royal Family are said to be creatures of habit and William and Kate are no exception.

If they like a holiday destination, they tend to return again and again … and again.

They adore skiing and take to the slopes regularly in Klosters and Courchevel, and occasionally in Verbier. But in spite of their love of winter sports, any of these resorts would be an unusual choice for a honeymoon. If past form is anything to go by, the destination could be any one of three sun-soaked locations.

Rodrigues Island near Mauritius cannot be ruled out after the couple enjoyed a relaxing summer break before their last year of university. William wrote his 10,000-word university dissertation about the island's coral reefs, and went there to study ocean currents with the Royal Geographical Society in 2000.

But the smart money is on one of two dream destinations. The white sand beaches and palm trees of deserted Desroches Island in the Seychelles are hard to beat. But one factor against Desroches is that William took Kate there shortly after getting back together from their split. The location may bring back some awkward memories from a tricky time in the relationship.

Which leaves the odds-on favourite as Mustique, an island adored both by showbiz royalty and the real thing. William and Kate went in Easter 2006 while he was on a break from Sandhurst and again

in August 2008 after he finished a month on a Navy warship. The destination has also been a favourite for Kate's family – but they are unlikely to join her for the honeymoon!

One place likely to be ruled out is Lewa Downs, the Kenyan nature reserve run by the family of Jecca Craig – once linked to William. And the safest bet of all? They won't be booking flights to Ibiza to spend a week in La Maison de Bang Bang. The £5-million villa where the couple stayed in 2006 is owned by Kate's uncle Gary Goldsmith.

12

The Future King and Queen

The nation's wait for the most hotly anticipated royal engagement in history finally came to an end shortly after 11 a.m. on Tuesday 16 November 2010. It triggered celebrations around the world and unprecedented coverage across newspapers, radio and TV stations.

Thoughtful William gave Kate his mother's cherished engagement ring so that Diana would be a special part of his happiest day. Kate wore the sapphire and diamond band as the couple faced the world for the first time as bride and groom-to-be. William explained: 'As you may have recognised, it's my mother's engagement ring. So of course it's very special to me and Kate's very special to me now as well – and it's only right the two are put together.

'It was my way of making sure my mother didn't miss out on today and the excitement and the fact we're going to spend the rest of our lives together.'

The couple discussed the ring as they posed for pictures amid an electrifying atmosphere in the Entrée Room at St James's Palace. It was the only deeply personal keepsake William asked for following Diana's death in a Paris car crash in 1997, when he was 15. He told his father, Prince Charles, he would one day like to use the band – a

' The couple discussed the ring as they posed for pictures amid an electrifying atmosphere in the Entrée Room at St James's Palace.'

physical link to his mother — for his own engagement. And he said it reflected a period in his parents' lives when they were truly happy.

William has stored it in a safe ever since but tucked it away in his rucksack when he went on holiday with Kate in Kenya in October. He refused to let anyone near the bag for fear of his secret being discovered. But when the time was right, he slipped it on Kate's finger after he popped the question and she said: 'Yes.'

Natural beauty Kate seemed overwhelmed with joy as she showed off the ring, which Diana had continued to wear after splitting with Charles until just before her death.

A happy quirk of fate meant it was a perfect fit, with no adjustments needed.

Prince Harry said he was 'delighted' by his brother's engagement. He added: 'It means I get a sister, which I have always wanted.'

In the Entrée Room, Kate looked stunning for her first appearance as the future Queen in a low-cut blue dress by her favourite designer, Issa. The ornate room was lit up by a battery of flashes from photographers' cameras. William jokingly told the snappers: 'I can't see any of you.'

Kate appeared nervous at first but soon composed herself as she said of William's proposal: 'It was very romantic and very personal.'

Asked if the Prince had gone down on one knee, he interrupted to say: 'That's going to stay a secret.'

But it is understood he did not strike the traditional pose at a location simply described as 'beautiful and remote'.

Kate tucked her left hand in Wills' right elbow as she admitted she felt some trepidation at becoming a Royal. Speaking softly, she said:

'It's quite a daunting prospect but hopefully I'll take it in my stride. And William's a great teacher so hopefully he'll be able to help me.'

Wills, looking smart in a Gieves and Hawkes suit, white Turnbull and Asser shirt and maroon tie, quipped: 'She's very good at flattery.'

The only time the Prince appeared to bridle was when he was asked why it had taken him and Kate so long to become engaged. 'I didn't realise it was a race,' he said, 'otherwise I probably would have been a lot quicker. But also the time is right now. We're both very happy and I'm very glad I have done it.'

A question about their love evoked memories of one put to Prince Charles when he became engaged to Diana, triggering his memorable response: 'Whatever love means.'

But William was much more at ease. He said: 'Where do we start? Obviously we both have a very fun time together, both have a very good sense of humour.

'We're down to earth, we take the mickey out of each other a lot, and she's got plenty of habits that make me laugh that I tease her about.'

Before the day of their announcement, only Kate's dad Michael knew about the engagement — although William had asked for his permission *after* he proposed. Prince Charles and the Queen were told early in the morning although they knew it was in the offing. The couple discussed their media strategy over how to announce the news with senior advisors at St James's Palace.

Brave Kate embarked on her first off-the-record 'meet and greet' with selected journalists before her first photo call. She came across as composed and friendly, if obviously jittery, and was said to be pleased with how her 'debut' had gone. She will now wind down her work with her parents' website Party Pieces.

Royal watchers then got their first chance to scrutinise Kate in a joint television interview with her future husband. ITV News political editor Tom Bradby — whose wife Claudia is a pal of Kate's — was handed the job of quizzing the couple at Clarence House. The couple proved remarkably candid in their first ever public chat as they were asked about the proposal.

'It was about three weeks ago on holiday in Kenya,' said William. 'We had a little private time away together with some friends. I just decided that it was the right time really.

'We'd been talking about marriage for a while so it wasn't a massively big surprise. I took her up somewhere nice in Kenya and I proposed.'

As Kate chimed in, millions of Britons heard their future Queen speak clearly for the first time — her answers in the televised press conference had been drowned out by the noise of camera shutters.

'It was very romantic,' she laughed. 'There's a true romantic in there.'

Bradby pushed her: 'So you said yes, obviously?'
Kate replied: 'Of course, yes.'
Like any normal young man, William was understandably nervous before taking the plunge. 'I'd been planning it for a while,' he explained, 'but as any guy out there will know, it takes a certain amount of motivation to get yourself going.'

Then, in an utterance that wrong-footed many Royal watchers, Kate insisted she didn't see it coming. 'I really didn't expect it at all,' she said. 'I thought he might have maybe thought about it, but no — it was a total shock when it came, and very exciting.'

She then confirmed that William had produced the ring. Running the precious moment back through his mind, William said: 'I had been carrying it around with me in my rucksack for about three weeks before that and I literally would not let it go. Everywhere I went I was keeping hold of it because I knew this thing, if it disappeared, I would be in a lot of trouble.

'You hear a lot of horror stories about proposing and things going horribly wrong. It went really, really well — and I was really pleased she said "Yes".'

The most touching part of the interview came as William opened his heart about the family heirloom he had given to Kate. 'It's my mother's engagement ring,' said William.

'I thought it was quite nice because obviously she [Diana] is not going to be around to share any of the fun and excitement of it all. This was my way of keeping her close to it all.'

He admitted he was no expert on jewellery but went on: 'I've been reliably informed it's a sapphire with some diamonds. I'm sure everyone recognises it from previous times.'

Seeing the impact of the emotion on her fiancé, Kate said: 'It's beautiful. I just hope I look after it. It's very, very special.'

William confirmed that the couple were happy about their news but admitted there were stresses behind the scenes. 'We're like sort of ducks,' he said, 'very calm on the surface with little feet going under the water.'

'We're both very happy and I'm very glad I have done it.'

Old-fashioned William revealed he had asked for Kate's dad Michael's permission after she had agreed to become his wife. He said: 'I was torn between asking Kate's dad first and then the realisation that he might actually say "No" dawned upon me. So I thought if I ask Kate first then he can't really say no.'

Kate told how mum Carole was 'absolutely over the moon', and spoke of the importance of her family. 'I hope we will be able to have a happy family ourselves,' she added.

Bradby took the initiative to ask if the couple wanted lots of children. William said cautiously: 'I think we'll take it one step at a time. We'll sort of get over the marriage first and then maybe look at the kids. But obviously we want a family so we'll have to start thinking about that.'

The couple also recounted their early years together at St Andrews.

'We were friends for over a year first and it just sort of blossomed from then on,' William said. 'We just spent more time with each other, had a good giggle, had lots of fun and realised we shared the same interests and had a really good time.

'She's got a really naughty sense of humour, which kind of helps me because I've got a really dry sense of humour. We had a really good laugh — and things happened.'

Asked about her first impression of William, Kate showed an endearing turn of self-deprecation. Turning her body to face him, she admitted: 'Well, I actually think I went bright red when I met you and sort of scuttled off, feeling very shy about meeting you.'

And she denied a story that she had William's picture on her wall at school — but not before William took the chance to gain some capital from it. 'There wasn't just one, there were about 20,' he joked.

But Kate stepped in: 'He wishes! No, I had the Levi's guy on my wall, not a picture of William, sorry.'

William refused to let it drop, saying: 'It was me in Levi's, honestly.'

He explained that the couple had moved in together at university as pals living with a couple of other students. Their relationship 'sort of blossomed from there', which he admitted surprised the other two chums.

Kate told how the second-in-line to the throne cooked for her regularly at university — but got frustrated if recipes went awry.

'He would always come with a bit of angst and a bit of anger if something had gone wrong,' she said. 'I would have to wander in and save something.'

William quipped: 'I would say I'm getting better at cooking. Kate would say I'm getting a lot worse.'

And he confessed that she had saved his bacon numerous times. 'When I was trying to impress Kate I was trying to cook these amazing fancy dinners,' he said, 'and what would happen was I would burn something, something would spill, something would catch on fire and she would be sitting in the background trying to help, and basically taking control of the whole situation, so I was quite glad she was there at the time.'

Kate disclosed that she had been 'quite nervous' about meeting Prince Charles but found him 'very, very welcoming, very friendly'.

And she told how she met the Queen at the 2008 wedding of Princess Anne's son, Peter Phillips, to his Canadian fiancée, Autumn Kelly.

'I first met her at Peter and Autumn's wedding,' she said, 'and again it was amongst a lot of other guests and she was very friendly.' William added: 'She had wanted to meet Kate for a while, so it was very nice for her to come over and say "Hello".'

The couple also confronted the thorny issue of their split, which William put down to youth. 'We were both finding ourselves as such and being different characters and stuff,' he said.

Kate said bravely: 'At the time I wasn't very happy about it, but actually it made me a stronger person.'

William told how his love for Kate had developed over time and hailed their time together as 'really fun'. He said:

'When I first met Kate I knew there was something very special about her. I knew there was possibly something that I wanted to explore there. We ended up being friends for a while and that was a good foundation.'

'We went through a few stumbling blocks as every relationship does, but we really picked ourselves up and carried on. It is just really

'It is just
really easy
being with
each other...'

easy being with each other. It is really fun — and I'm extremely funny,' he joked, 'and she loves that, so it's been good.'

He blamed the length of time it had taken him to formalise the relationship on his job. 'I had my military career,' he said, 'and I really wanted to concentrate on my flying. I couldn't have done this if I was still doing my training.'

Kate was asked about Princess Diana — the woman with whom she will inevitably face comparison. She said:

'I would have loved to have met her and she's obviously an inspirational woman to look up to. You know, it is a wonderful family — the members I've met have achieved a lot.'

William instantly stepped in to to protect Kate, saying: 'There's no pressure. Like Kate said it is about carving your own future. No one is trying to fill my mother's shoes. What she did was fantastic.

'It's about making your own future and your own destiny. Kate will do a very good job of that. I wanted to give her a chance to see in and to back out if she needed to before it all got too much. I'm trying to learn from the past. I just wanted to give her the best chance to settle in and to see what happens on the other side.'

The historic interview finished with the couple speaking of their excitement and nerves at what the future holds. 'We are hugely excited,' said William, 'and looking forward to spending the rest of our lives together.'

With an eye to her future public role, Kate said: 'It's obviously nerve-racking. I don't know the ropes. William is obviously used to it. But I'm willing to learn quickly and work hard. I really hope I can make a difference, even in the smallest way. I am looking forward to helping as much as I can.'

The wedding will be held in London in 2011 on a date still to be fixed as this book went to press. Afterwards they will live at the farmhouse in Anglesey, North Wales, where William has been based for the last few months for his work as a search and rescue pilot at RAF Valley.

It has been a long haul for William and Kate but they have finally made a lifelong commitment to each other. Delighted Britons and Royal watchers across the globe are certain it will prove to be a happy one.